Relax

Create

Enjoy

What is a Mandala?

The word Mandala is Sanskrit for "circle."
Mandalas are a representation of the universe
in many belief systems.
They are used in sacred rituals as a
spiritual guidance tool, as an aid for meditation
and to establish a sacred space.
Some traditions create mandalas using sand
to express the impermanent nature of existence.
Creating (or colouring) a mandala calms the
mind and body, releases stress and anxiety,
boosts creativity and opens the
path to spiritual growth.

Most of all it's fun!

The deep roots never doubt spring will come.

Marty Rubin

In the depth of winter I finally learned that
there was in me an invincible summer.

Albert Camus

Delicious autumn! My very soul is wedded to it, and
if I were a bird I would fly about the Earth
seeking the successive autumns.

George Eliot

When the sun is shining I can do anything;
No mountain is too high, no trouble too difficult to overcome.

Wilma Rudolph

Spring is the mischief in me.

Robert Frost

It's always summer somewhere.

Lily Pulitzer

I loved autumn, the season of the year
that God seemed to have put there just for the beauty of it.

Lee Maynard

No snowflake ever falls in the wrong place.

Zen and the Art of Happiness

The earth laughs in flowers.

Ralph Waldo Emerson

If you're not barefoot, then you're overdressed.

Unknown

I hope I can be the autumn leaf, who looked at the sky and lived.
And when it was time to leave, gracefully it knew life was a gift.

Dodinsky

The color of springtime is in the flowers,
the color of winter is in the imagination.

Terri Guillemets

If you look the right way, you can see that
the whole world is a garden.

Frances Hodgson Burnett

A perfect summer day is when the sun is shining,
the breeze is blowing, the birds are singing,
and the lawnmower is broken.

James Dent

In summer, the song sings itself.

William Carlos Williams

My old grandmother always used to say,
'Summer friends will melt away like summer snows,
but winter friends are friends forever'.

George R.R. Martin

Happiness held is the seed; Happiness shared is the flower.

John Harrigan

Autumn carries more gold in its pocket
than all the other seasons.

Jim Bishop

Fall has always been my favorite season.
The time when everything bursts with its last beauty,
as if nature had been saving up all year for the grand finale.

Lauren De Stefano

And don't think the garden loses its ecstasy in winter.
It's quiet, but the roots are down there riotous.

Rumi

To plant a garden is to believe in tomorrow.

Audrey Hepburn

Live in the sunshine. Swim in the sea. Drink in the wild air.

Ralph Waldo Emerson

Autumn is a second spring when every leaf is a flower.

Albert Camus

Snowflakes are one of nature's most fragile things
but just look what they can do when they stick together.

Vesta M. Kelly

Seasons change, and so do we.

Nikki Che

Smell the sea, and feel the sky. Let your soul and spirit fly.

Van Morrison

Another fall, another turned page...

Wallace Stegner

That's what winter is: an exercise in remembering how
to still yourself then how to come pliantly back to life again.

Ali Smith

An optimist is the human personification of spring.

Susan J. Bissonette

Let us dance in the sun, wearing wild flowers in our hair...

Susan Polis Schutz

How beautifully leaves grow old!
How full of light and color are their last days!

John Burroughs

They who sing through the summer must dance in the winter.

Italian Proverb

We might think we are nurturing our garden
but of course it's our garden that is really nurturing us.

Jenny Uglow

Potential is like a summer crop.
If it don't rain, it don't grow.

Charles Oakley

Autumn is the mellower season,
and what we lose in flowers we more than gain in fruits.

Samuel Butler

What good is the warmth of summer, without the
cold of winter to give it sweetness.

John Steinbeck

A flower blossoms for its own joy.

Oscar Wilde

There shall be eternal summer in the grateful heart.

Celia Thaxter

Autumn shows us how beautiful it is to let things go.

Unknown

In winter, I plot and plan. In spring, I move.

Henry Rollins

A kind word is like a spring day.

Russian Proverb

Summer afternoon – summer afternoon; to me
those have always been the two most beautiful words
in the English language.

Henry James

Everyone must take time to sit and watch the leaves turn.

Elizabeth Lawrence

Snow flurries began to fall and they swirled
around people's legs like house cats. It was magical,
this snow globe world.

Sarah Addison Allen

Don't wait for someone to bring you flowers.
Plant your own garden and decorate your own soul.

Luther Burbank

Some of the best memories are made in flip-flops.

Kellie Elmore

Autumn is the season to find contentment at home
by paying attention to what we already have.

Unknown

How many lessons of faith and beauty we should lose,
if there were no winter in our year!

Thomas Wentworth Higginson

Sometimes we can only find our true direction when we let
the wind of change carry us.

Mimi Novic

Rise above the storm and you will find the sunshine.

Mario Fernandez

Printed in Great Britain
by Amazon

37640121R00057